From The Heart
By Patricia Butler

"FROM THE HEART", VOLUME ONE BY PATRICIA BUTLER (2)
© COPYRIGHT 2021, PATRICIA BUTLER

ALL RIGHTS RESERVED. NO PART OF THIS PUBLICATION MAY BE REPRODUCED, STORED IN A RETRIEVAL SYSTEM OR TRANSMITTED IN ANY FORM OR BY ANY MEANS ELECTRONIC, MECHANICAL, PHOTOCOPY, RECORDING OR ANY OTHER——EXCEPT FOR BRIEF QUOTATIONS IN PRINTED REVIEWS, WITHOUT THE PRIOR PERMISSION OF THE AUTHOR.

ISBN: 978-1-7368064-0-1

LIBRARY OF CONGRESS NO: 2021904414

FOR MORE INFORMATION ABOUT "FROM THE HEART" AND THE POEMS BY PATRICIA BUTLER, OR **TO ORDER ADDITIONAL COPIES**, PLEASE VISIT: **WWW.PATRICIABUTLERPOEMS.COM** OR CALL **(931) 255-1349**

PAINTERS DREAM PRODUCTIONS IS A BOOK PUBLISHER DEDICATED TO PROVIDING PUBLISHING SERVICES AT AFFORDABLE PRICES HELPING TO ELEVATE OUR AUTHORS WORK.

HTTPS://WWW.PAINTERSDREAM.COM | 931-304-1359

Website Design | Audio Video Production | Social Media Marketing | Book Publishing

Prologue

Completing a book is like taking a beautiful piece of material and deciding exactly where to cut, when to cut and what to cut. One wants a beautiful tapestry design when finished, but decisions along the way can make the design different.

I want to salute my dear friends who made this adventure so pleasant. Thank you for not complaining when I cut the fabric wrong but celebrating when the fabric went together appropriately.

I confess that every poem written here has been coauthored by God and me. God gave me the gift to write poetry, but He authored the poems. I may have put the words on paper, but He gave me the words to write. Hopefully the poems will touch your heart in such a way that you are more caring, loving, and humble in every way.

Although many touched my life through the years, and made me aware of feelings and tears, I want to explain that there are folks that I know, who have been filled with God's Spirit and helped me grow.

All is evident through the poems you see I wrote poems for whatever happened to be. God was in charge and He instructed me, Cause He wanted to share in His glory.

So a prologue would include so many names That I could not include all of the same; however, I'm thankful for all I've acquired to use my poems to help others to be inspired.

I appreciate my friends who have helped me learn; Through the trials, the testing and the daily turn that gifts are given for all to use whatever they are, them you can lose.

To my publisher, Perry Hartman, you do more than organize, design, guide, and publish. You make God proud of all you do.

To my husband, what else can I say? You greet me every morning, keep me on my toes, and are still "my knight in shining armor." You are the sparkle in my life and you are a born-again Christian.

To my family I salute you for accepting me unconditionally.

Finally, I salute the readers. You have entrusted me with your most valuable asset – your time. It is my prayer that God will touch your heart with the poems, and that you will realize the tapestry of material is His to behold.

God speaks daily through coincidence, it's clear;
So be alert to His biddings and you will always bring cheer;
Cause God will tell you what you are to do,
If only you are alert and listening, it's true.

Mr. & Mrs. Butler

After Thoughts Related to Macau

Life is filled with many curves and turns
And decisions we make become lessons that we learn.
Touching the lives of people in Macau, so far away
Reminded me that life must be lived day by day.
Listening to God to know His perfect plan,
For our lives minute to minute and man to man.
Each word, each deed, each thought and action we complete,
Is like the ripples in a pond caused by a feat
Of throwing a simple stone into a body of water,
And allowing the chain reaction to grow
To the edge of that water.
We often change the future of may we see,
And seldom notice because we are so busy.
The people of Macau certainly need our prayer,
And God's work is growing day by day there.
However, I fear the USA has saddened God's heart,
Because from God's teachings we seem apart.
We have only one Christian in every ten men.
And it appears quite popular to flaunt one's sin,
Without repentance and blinded eyes to see
Without forgiveness of God's love, the key.
There are many in Cookeville without the Lord in their life.
Whose world is filled with constant strife.
We may be the only light they may see today,
So as we walk throughout life let's pray
For those people we pass along the way.
We may be the only one that's ever thought to say,
A prayer for those people we see along the way.
That prayer may make a difference in that person's life someday.

An Apprentice

A YOUNG MAN ATTENDED OUR CHURCH AS MANY OFTEN DO.
HE ALSO ATTENDED TECH WHERE HE STUDIED MUSIC AND OTHER THINGS TOO.
OUR CHURCH DECIDED TO REACH OUT TO THOSE AT THE UNIVERSITY,
TO PROVIDE AN APPRENTICE JOB IN MUSIC FOR OUR COMMUNITY.

JOSH WAS SELECTED TO FILL THAT NEEDED EMPTY SPACE,
AND TO HELP JONATHON IN EVERY MINISTERIAL PLACE.
BY TEACHING, DIRECTING, LISTENING AND AIDING IN THE RACE TO
COMPLETE THE MANY TASKS THAT A MUSIC MINISTER MUST EMBRACE.

JOSH GREW HIS PEOPLE SKILLS THROUGH REVELATIONAL INSIGHTS,
TO TOUCH THE HEARTS OF THOSE HE'D MET WITH JOYFUL DELIGHT.
HE LEAD THE ORCHESTRA, THE YOUTH GROUP, AND THE CHOIR TOO.
HE SANG, PLAYED DUETS, AND EVEN PLAYED IN TEBACHIHO, ITS TRUE.

HE MINISTERED TO EVERYONE IN MANY ENCOURAGING WAYS
WITH A JOYFUL, WILLING SPIRIT AND MUCH GODLY PRAISE.
BUT AS WITH LIFE WHEN LIVES TOUCH EACH OTHER ON THIS EARTH;
THINGS OFTEN CHANGE AND PARTING HAPPENS MANY TIMES AFTER BIRTH.

THE TIME HAS COME FOR JOSH TO MOVE TO SEMINARY TO GROW.
FOR GOD TO USE IN OTHER WAYS THAT WE CANNOT POSSIBLY KNOW;
BUT OUR LIVES HAVE BEEN IMPRINTED WITH THIS SPECIAL SPIRIT-FILLED MAN,
AND WE PRAY THAT OUR PATHS MAY CROSS MANY TIMES AGAIN.

Angels
(A Song Too!)

Do you believe in Angels or think that they're fantasy?
The Bible says that they are real, they're as real as you and me.
There was a mighty battle in heaven long ago some angels fought
with God or so the story goes.

God and His best angels triumphed in the end
He kicked them out of Heaven and to Hades did send.
An angel appeared to Mary and told her of a birth.
How she would bear the Savior, bringing glory to the Earth.

When Christ was born in Bethlehem, a star shone high above.
The angles sang so joyously, they heralded His great love.
As Jesus grew tired and weary, the Angels drew near the man.
They ministered as best they could, while He fulfilled God's plan.

The family sadly mourned His death,
The grave could not conceal.
Christ is risen! He's alive!
They proclaimed with mighty zeal.

They say all the Angels rejoice, each time a soul is saved.
They're dancing on the streets of Gold, which are so richly paved.
Although we rarely see them, they're busy at their task.
A protecting of God's children we don't even have to ask.

Be kind to everyone we meet, dine with strangers if you dare.
For they say that some of those who do meet angles unaware.
And if your death angel tarries, the next sound you may hear
Is the shout of the Arch Angel when Jesus Christ appears.

Baby Dyer

We hear there's a new fellow due in this town,
Who will bring joy and laughter to all who're around.
He'll be entering the house of Dyer, they say,
With parents, John and Becky, showing him the way.

He is a blessing and gift from our God above,
Designed to fill their house with his tender love;
As he grows from diapers to a black tux someday,
And learns about God's love and humor along the way.

Many lives will touch his special page;
As folks write their comments on the latest rage.
There is one thing about him we know for sure,
He'll be loved, encouraged, and taught to endure.

Whatever God holds in store for his days.
As his tapestry is sewn in multicolored ways,
By grandparents, relatives and friends who share.
As he enters this world, they all add their prayers.

Dyer Family: Alex, Josh, (Buddy), Nathan. Nathan's beginning will be in Volume 2.

Calamity

He trudged down the road in a labored ole' way.
He was hoping that the way would end today.
He heard some shots that seemed that far away,
And prayed for his buddies to be okay.

The cold in the air was much chill to bear,
And his gray tattered jacket had many a tear.
His boots had holes for the chill to creep in.
And he hadn't a blanket to help him, my friend.

He'd thought this war would be over and done.
Then in a few weeks life would be as it begun;
But, the war had hung on way too long.
Folks and land had been ravaged with many a wrong.

He had an old hat that still covered his head,
As though warmth could be there as he tread.
Through the brambles, bushes and wooded site
To find his buddies and help with the fight.

What was that sound he heard to the right?
Was it another soldier to join in the fight,
Or was it animals in the woods at daylight,
Or was it his hunger laying tricks of fright.

Then a burst of sound filled his being
A light from the right entered his seeing.
A pressure hit his body with a mighty force,
And he fell to the ground blood running its course.

He lay very still as he thought of his life.
His state, his farm, his children, his wife,
Would he see them again on this side of the river
Or would he die soon with a moan and quiver.

Later he heard someone approaching very quietly,
For he heard a twig snap, leaves move and a bird flee.
It was a young boy with an old flint rifle
Dragging a body and with tears–trying to stifle.

He rushed to my side to check on me
His suit was gray as mine was, you see
I looked very closely at the lad so near,
And wondered why a lad so young was here.

He told me he was looking for brother and dad.
He'd found his brother on a dirt pad.
He's crossed the river many days before.
Cause flies and such covered his body galore.

He was headed for home to bury him there
Then happened upon me on the ground bare
He made me comfortable in every way
Left his brother there to rush for help that day.

My story isn't finished — in review,
I lived to see my family anew
But how many men wearing gray
Lay in a field in such a way.

It saddens me when I think of those days,
Where life in the South changed in many ways.
The world today continues to be
Paying the price for the calamity.

Carly Beth Butler

A new baby was about to arrive.
Rhett and Adrienne knew it would be alive.
The minutes were dancing by, it seems,
"The arrival was coming soon," says the team.

After fifteen hours of labor, oh me,
A new baby was soon to be.
With black curly hair she came into view
At 3:17 after a struggle or few.

Carly Beth Butler arrived in tow,
With Grandmothers there to see the show.
A prettier baby they'd never seen.
It caused them to glow just like a queen.

Her fingers were perfect as well as her toes
Her face was red but beautiful, and even her nose.
Was perfect and a gift for all to see,
She will be God's instrument for all glory.

She was named and her birth date revealed.
As January 7, 2009. It is sealed.
Proud parents, Rhett and Adrienne
Were blessed with a girl, Amen and Amen.

Members from each family group completed a block by sewing the pictures. After returning the piece, it was made for Carly.

Four Generations
Arbie Bowen (Mimi), Rhett holding Carly Beth, & Adrienne

Christian Fruits

What's this thing called, "Christian,"
and what does it mean?
What makes one different
from other people I've seen.

The fruits of the Spirit
make more Christians cool.
The fruits are the products
of following God's rule.

It doesn't mean they're better,
only redeemed, you see.
Because they love Jesus
who died for you and me.

Their faces show peace, joy,
kindness and love.
Their actions so faithful are
guided from above.

Patience, gentleness and
self-control too,
The fruits of the spirit
should always shine through.

Dominica

On March the second in 2007, a group of singers left for Atlanta. Our mission was to share the love of Jesus in Dominica. After a quick night's rest, we rushed to the airport for a flight. Thank the Lord, security, customs, bag weight, and plastic containers were all alright.

A night was spent in Barbados to change to a smaller, less luxurious size plane. And we learned that island time is a little more laid back and not always the same. But arrival in Dominica happened without much alarm. With a fast trip to Deliverance Church in a setting filled with charm.

The church ladies provided a typical Dominican menu with chicken, juice, fruit, vegetables, and choices were many, not few. After eating our fill, preparations were made for the church meeting. With hand chimes ringing, the choir singing and Steve Evangicube leading.

The church had planned for our visit as well. With a skit by the youth on God's way or hell. The entire service was energizing and a blessing. With testimonies, rhythmic music and the pastor teaching.

As the week unfolded blessings did abound. As the group sang, witnessed, and walked throughout the town. Opportunities were abundant through many avenues with music as the vehicle to open doors to choose.

Faith, salvation and Jesus' love for eternity. Or rejection, nonbelief, and soul poverty. Singing in markets, radio stations, churches, hospitals – what a joy! In airports, hotel, in the medical center, and on streets – oh boy!

Using evangicubes to relate God's gift to all, lives were changed when many answered God's call, by praying the sinners' prayer and feeling anew many new Christians were Added - Hallelu!

Changes happened often as each day progressed, but joy filled our hearts through the entire process. Because as the song we sang states loud and clear, we are never alone what should we fear?

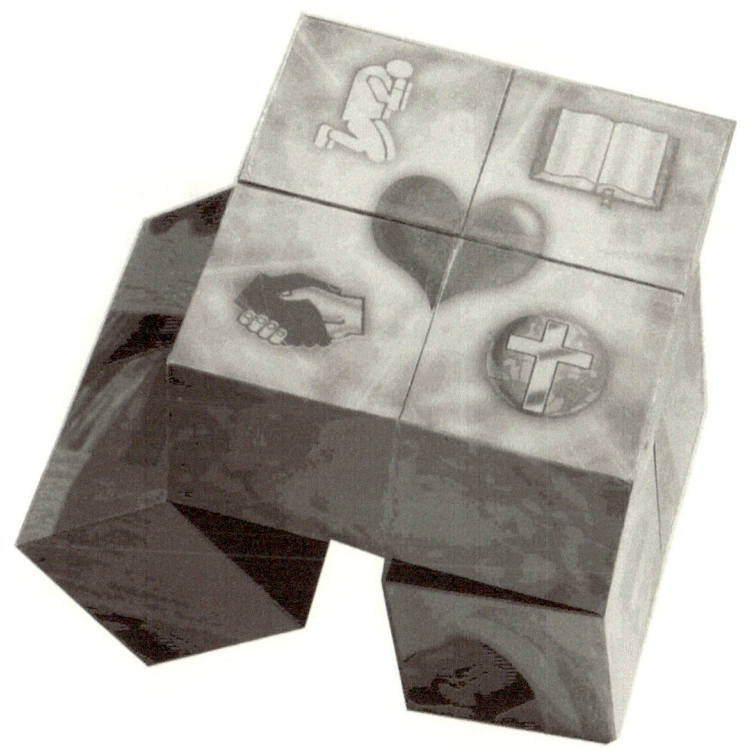

This Evangicube led many people to the Lord.
As we were leaving, the newly saved boys
we're waving to us and said, "see you in Heaven!"

Do We Look For Another?

While in prison John asked Jesus the question in wonder,
"Art thou he that should come, or do we look for another?"
The question remains, "Is Jesus God's son?"
Jesus gave the answer to show John that he was the one
Look at my credentials observed by others and told.
And then compare them to those mentioned by Isaiah of old.
The blind could see, the lame could walk.
The lepers were cleansed as all did talk.
The deaf could hear, the dead were raised.
The poor the gospel could hear and praise.

Today in our world there are religious leaders like wells.
Some that are full and some as dry as the fires of hell.
Although these leaders have known the righteous way.
Some have not escaped the pollution of the world today.
In the Bible, David, the one after God's own heart
Killed and lusted and from God did depart.
Darkness of heart and agony and pain
Awakened his soul to the God he had shamed.
Soon his confession was given for sin.
He pleaded and repented deep from within.

Christ's reflection like a mirror I see
And I look at my life compared to He
Woe is my heart as I see how I've failed,
But great is my joy for his grace prevails.
With faith I look forward to His second coming,
And fear there are others to whom I should be running.
Because their lives are dry and their joy withheld.
Since they do not know Christ, nor His hands with the nail.
The joy of Christmas is the expression of love
That each person experiences through God above.
Do we look for another remains the cry?
No, Christ is risen and His return is nigh.

For if we believe that Jesus died and rose from the dead, so also God will bring with Him those who have fallen asleep through Jesus. - **1 Thessalonians 4:14**

Now may the God of peace, who brought up from the dead the great Shepherd of the sheep through the blood of the eternal covenant, that is, Jesus our Lord. - **Hebrews 13:20**

Do You Know My Savior?

Do you know my Savior, my Abba, my Lord?
He loves you beyond imagination; you are adored.
He longs to communicate and guide you day by day,
But you must decide to listen and seek His only way.

If you open your heart, He will draw you near.
Because He created you for fellowship with Him, that's clear;
He longs to use you in His mighty way
But you must be willing to sacrifice your life each day.

The world doesn't mind a Sunday, lukewarm Christian;
But it fears a righteous one that's in God's transition.
If you look with the eyes of your heart at our Savior,
One cannot doubt His love by His own behavior.

Have you helped others with love's motive in mind
To have them treat you hatefully and very unkind?
Have you felt the pain of the cross He moved
Or felt the hatred of those who boo——ed?

Can you feel the sting of the whip on His back
When He stumbled as you hear the whip again crack?
Have you felt His nail-scarred hands and felt His pain
With the hammered spikes that were bloodstained?

Have you ached as you were mocked with a thorny crown
As the blood dripped down your face and laughter did sound?
Have you had a thirst quenched, not with water or wine;
But with vinegar so bitter tears formed in your eyes?

Have you felt the weight on your hands nailed to the cross, and
Been humbled as though everything you were was lost?
Have you felt that you could not endure any more pain,
And then prayed for those who treated you so insane?

Jesus endured all the sacrifices above
Because He cared about us with unconditional love.
He wants us to become a living sacrifice for Him
If we want a relationship centered in Him.

Our purpose on earth is to glorify our Savior,
And we can do that only by our decisive behavior
As we fellowship with Him day by day
And follow His footsteps as He shows the way.

The choice remains in whatever we do,
But the price of our decision will be eternal too.
Do you know my Savior and Lord today?
If not, why not ask Him to show you His way?

For He is the Potter, and we are the clay.
He wants to shape your life and mine today.
If we take our wounds to Jesus and become stewards of our pain.
He will change our scars with His love through His blood stains.

Do you know my Savior, my Abba, my Lord?
He loves you beyond imagination; you are adored.
He longs to hold you and heal your pain,
But you must reach out to Him and call His name.

Evelyn Mae Butler's Birth

It is hard to believe, but I wouldn't jive,
Evelyn Mae Butler was born August 31, 2005;
In a hospital in Livingston, Tennessee,
With her Mom and Dad for the world to see.

I was called immediately as I had asked to be;
Cause I was teaching in Baxter, a long way from the baby.
I was informed earlier to make my way;
Because the baby was about to be born, Hooray!

I rushed in the door, found Father with baby in hand.
He called to me quickly and asked me to stand,
And watch the nurse as she cleaned the child;
While he went to take care of Mom, in her own style.

The nurse said that Evelyn was doing just great.
She completed those things a newborn needs on that date.
She had all her fingers and her toes.
Her face was reddish, even her nose.

She had a little hair upon her head,
And she was precious even in her bed.
Her Mom suddenly appeared on the scene,
Pushed in wheelchair by hubby, and looking like a queen.

Later that day, her Grand Mother Peggy arrived.
She entered the room with sister and flowers alive.
Kaylynn was introduced to her new friend,
A sister for life, from now to the end.

Faith

So many things in life we do
require a choice by me or you.
We choose to be happy or to be sad,
we choose to be joyful or to be mad.

When life sends us detours or some strife,
we choose a new road for our present life.
We strive to find any easy route;
but God often sends many a doubt.

We take a step and look quickly around
no problems lurk so we continue down.
The path we have taken step-by-step;
and pray the route is the right one kept.

The days pass by and soon the years,
we've endured sickness, health, joys and tears.
He guides our thoughts day-by-day
and cleans up our messes in His own way.

So faithful to Him we will continue to be;
For He guides our life for all to see.
He takes our sins and turns them around,
to make His tapestry beautifully bound.

Faith is Putting Belief into Action

Fifty Years

Hooray! Ole! And give a shout!
The Fitts' are ready to celebrate, no doubt.
They've been married for fifty full, long years;
And have loved each other through laughter and tears.

They met at Murray State most folks say;
And decided to tie the knot one special day.
The wedding date was set in 1959.
The month of January because the right time.

After this special event occurred.
They moved to an apartment, that's what I heard.
They stayed there 'til Gerald graduated from Murray State
And started their journey to this present date.

Their lives have been filled with many roads,
Some to Breckenridge and some to other abodes.
But they settled in Poseyville, Indiana, you see
To raise their own beautiful family.

A boy named Allen arrived, not a minute too late
In the month of March in 1968.
And what do you know the stork again came.
A girl was born in 1970 and Lisa is her name.

With parents to tend and children to train
Time was valued more precious than fame
Their concern and love for friends and family
Endeared them to both eternally.

The days have come, and the days have gone,
And their lives have been filled with many a song.
Like piano lessons and hammers that ring,
Basketballs, boats and the whole water scene.

They've travelled to Europe and USA parts
They've cried, they laughed and felt with their heart.
As they stepped each day from song to song
Always loving their family when right or when wrong.

We tip our hats to the couple today
To salute fifty years of marriage their way.
And thank them for their example we see
As the hope for future generations' tenacity.

Marilyn & Gerald
50th Anniversary

From The Heart

Days will come and days will disappear,
As they fly more quickly with each passing year.
The days melt into a life of purpose or veneer,
Determined by each person who's allowed to steer.

The world has seen men considered great by their profession,
Where money and fame become an obsession.
For a life directed by the person's own design
Loses purpose without the plans God originally assigned.

Missions in your lives have always played a strong beat,
As you've touched lives while serving at Jesus' feet.
I pray God will keep you tightly held in His hand,
And use your efforts across many, many lands.

Lots of love to both of you.

Ed and Patricia Butler
Jeremiah 29:11

"Those who bring sunshine to the lives of others cannot keep it from themselves."

Gifts

I looked at the orchestra as it practiced one day,
And thought about each instrument and the sound it would play.
Each instrument capable as a soloist to be,
But when played together, it seemed a glimpse of glory touched me.

The combined timbres were such a delight,
Then I realized that the Master touched the music that night.
He made it quite clear as I devoured the piece.
That the gifts of each instrument were vital to the feast.

Then I thought Paul and the gifts one receives,
When becoming a Christian who truly believes.
The gifts as with the instruments are unique to each soul,
And given for the purpose to enhance the whole.

The Body of God's people working as one humble entity
Can glorify our precious Lord in a combined unity.
To provide not only salt, but a powerful light
For folks on this earth both day and night.

And as with the music God touched that day,
The Body will be joined by the Master some way.
To produce an orchestration for the world to see,
And glorify the Father which is our purpose to be!

Gordon Who?

We received an invite to a party today
It's to celebrate Gordon Vasseur's big birthday.
Sixty candles the big cake they will light
While friends and laughter will fill the night.

Who is this man named Gordon we know,
Who travels the world with balloons to blow?
He was born in Canada in Forty-Five,
And was raised in Michigan, oh my!

He became a citizen of the USA
Long after his twenty-first birthday.
His first job lasted thirty-three years
As an engineer for Michigan Bell, give cheers!

His life continued in a normal progression.
With marriage, children and church as sections.
There were ups and downs for all those years;
But God with His hands wiped those Vasseur tears.

He blessed them throughout their lives each day,
And retirement arrived in a strange, special way.
So Gordon's family gathered their earthly possessions.
They moved to Cookeville at their present location.

So who is the man who is becoming sixty?
A grandad, a media expert, and a clown that's nifty.
An electrician, a chauffeur, and a world-wide changer.
As a short-term missionary for the Christ of the manger.

He is a friend to all in numerous ways,
And he shows God's love most of these days.
As he walks through countries all over the world,
And spreads God's light to every boy and girl.

Gordon helped in the Classroom.
He has helped throughout the Community.

Grains of Sand

I heard someone laugh the other day;
And say, "How quickly life does fray!"
One day we're dating and on the phone.
The next we are married and staying at home.

Our choices for life are fast and new.
We grow and develop in character too.
There are joys and sorrows and often pains
As we wonder and ponder why so often it rains.

God in His love for you and for me
Chooses to develop us for His eternity.
There are days that are glorious in every way.
We'd like it to be that way every day.

Then days arrive with loss, illness and pain
For those that we love as our pillows grow tear-stained.
We feel lonely and angry in so many ways,
Cause deep down inside we want things our way.

But God in His wisdom reaches into our hearts
To fill it with love that He alone can impart.
He wraps His arms around us so very tight
That we feel the joy of glory a little more each night.

He helps us adjust to the pain of this life.
He dries our tears and soothes our inner strife.
He fills the emptiness in our daily routines
Like adding grains of sand on a lonely beach scene.

With each new deposit in heaven above
God draws us much closer to His abiding love.
We miss our loved ones with each daily breath;
But know God has plans for each person's death.

HE ALSO HAS PLANS FOR THOSE LEFT ON THIS EARTH
TO ACCOMPLISH A TASK THAT HE WANTS TO BIRTH.
OF COURSE HE USES PEOPLE TO HELP WITH THE DEED.
YOU MUST BE ON THE LIST OF ONE HE WILL NEED.

*Do not fear, for I am with you; do not be afraid, for I am your God.
I will strengthen you, I will also help you, I will also uphold you with
My righteous right hand. - Isaiah 41:10*

Happy Birthday
Adrienne Smith Butler

September 26, 2018

Birthdays come and birthdays go,
But really forty is special, you know.
Sometimes we are proud we made it long.
Others wonder if all that has been done is wrong.

You, my friend, have nothing to fear,
For each day you grow stronger in our Lord, so near.
You've always been in His tender care,
And He is growing your future for more to chair.

He knows you've been faithful to family and friends
And that your children are important to Him.
A wonderful helpmate and companion you've been,
Most times in most things without and within.

Whether rich or poor, you always abide.
And are willing to struggle when things are maligned.
You wait on the Lord and His will you seek,
Cause you know His path is for the meek.

Thank you for being like a daughter to us,
Always there to help as well as to trust.
Sharing your children throughout the year,
Listening to your husband through your tears.

Life is filled with ups and downs,
And as humans we have battles to abound.
God wants us to learn lessons of all kinds,
And often allows things to interrupt our minds.

Regardless of the human troubles we all endure,
There is one thing that is for sure.
God is in charge of all that we do,
And He has a plan for each one to do.

Thank you for continuing to search for His plan,
And for the woman you are becoming as His fan.
You may not be Ruth, or Esther, or Sarah,
But you are God's child and He alone knows His plan.

So follow Him closely each and every day,
And remember to listen only for your way,
Cause the next forty years may be your best,
And He may have only been putting you to the test!!!

William Rhett Butler Family
Adrienne, Rhett, Carly, & Gibbs

Happy Birthday
Rhett Butler
June 5, 2018

When we think of all that you've become.
We don't know how to add the sum.
Things that you touch, God usually grows.
He guides your life and your faith He knows.

He has given you a wife who loves you, its clear,
As well as a girl and a boy who love you so dear.
How blessed you are in so many ways,
That money can't buy in any number of days.

He is teaching you patience at this time,
And will bless you very soon beyond a find.
He knows the desires your heart would enjoy,
But He knows you will wait for His word to employ.

Forty is really a neat age to be,
Cause there are answers to some of life's mysteries.
But you seem to understand all of this too,
Cause the love of God requires obedience, its true.

You strive to follow His word always,
But evil sometimes causes a single sway,
In your plans, but you listen to our God,
Cause you know He will soon give you a nod.

You are a blessing to those you know,
And we're proud of all the ways you grow.
We look forward to the years to be,
Cause God has plans for all to see!!!

Heaven's Gift of Love

I woke up this very morning
Thinkin' 'bout that Christmas Day
With the baby in the manger
And his head upon the hay.

With the animals around him
And the angels from above
Sent to guard that little baby,
Who was heaven's gift of love.

Jesus was that little baby
Born in Bethlehem that day
With a birth so very humble
God's own son given Christmas Day.

Let's all lift our hearts to praise Him
Thanking heaven up above
For the gift of our own Savior
And for his own precious love.

Did you know that Mary had a baby?
And He is the Savior of the world.
Je-sus!, Je-sus!, Je-sus!

For unto you is born this day in the city of David a Saviour, which is Christ the Lord.
(Luke 2:11)

I'm Just A Sinner Saved By Grace

It is funny how we learn things and what remains in our minds.
As down through the ages some memories don't fade with time.
I recall very clearly a class over fifty years ago,
And a teacher revealing a birth that happened ages ago.

Now birthdays are important cause we all like to celebrate; But
this particular birth had a very significant date.
Because this precious baby in a stable of hay,
Would save this sinful world in a very special way.

I recall the questions that flooded my youthful mind,
And wondered how it covered the heavenly sky so.
Then a question popped into my mind with quickness of sound, "What
do wise men look like and how did they ever find the town?"

Then I stood outside and looked above,
I saw the stars that filled the sky like missions of hovering doves.
Then I wondered with a question as the stars I could see,
"Am I looking at the one that led folks to the baby?".

Even shepherds followed that bright special star,
Some were from near and some from afar.
The question came to my mind on that very day,
"How did they know the twinkling light led that way.

To the one who would love souls like no other,
And give commands to all to love each other.
As a youth my mind was filled with questions anew,
But one thing the teacher told clearly, and it's true.

"This baby was God's son of that no one should doubt,
And would grow to be a man as God worked things out."
His name was Jesus, and he would walk on this earth,
For thirty-three years from this humbly, lowly birth.

He'd heal the sick, the blind, the lame,
and other physical ailments one could name.
He could also heal the hearts of all kings of men,
from feelings and thoughts and actions of sin.

If He was given that special opportunity,
and invited to enter one's redeemed heart, you see.
Yes that day in the class as I listened amazed,
I felt a changing in my heart as I praised.

The forgiveness of my sins as tears flooded my eyes,
and a filling of God's presence — what a joyful surprise!
On that day as I heard Mrs. Kidd's words wisely ring,
I became a child in the class of the one and only King.

I'm thankful for His faithfulness throughout the years,
and pray He will be glorified in my laughter and tears.
I've continued to have questions about this special deal,
but I know that my relationship with Jesus is real.

And when I meet Him in glory face to face,
I will thank Him for His love, His mercy and grace.
He offers that to each and everyone
cause that's why He sacrificed His only son.

Do you know my Jesus, my Savior, my King?
He is my basketball star in the center ring,
He loves you whether the game you win or lose.
But you must decided that it is Him you choose.

I am just a sinner saved by grace — Grace is like getting a trophy you didn't really win. I don't deserve to be saved for my sins, but I am — and you can be also.

James Lee Butler & Jennifer Foust's Wedding

Everyone was excited because there was about to be,
A wedding in the unbelievable Butler family.
James Lee Butler and Jennifer Foust were about to do
What has been done for ages through and through.

The date was October and the year 2007.
They had known each other since before they were eleven,
They were friends through high school, that's for sure,
And marriage is now a process to endure.

The ushers, Turner and Billy, were busy as bees,
Seating folks everywhere as though they were keys,
To a puzzle put together for all to see;
Then suddenly there were folks they seated, oh me.

The ushers finally placed everyone in location,
And people were in the correct formation.
The coordinator, Becky Dyer, got the wedding party in place
And even had the Bride ready in her lace.

The music started and the bridesmaid came down the aisle.
They were Nickie, Darlene, and Lisa in style.
They lead the way to the future coming near
With groomsmen : Edward II, Rhett, and Edward, in front, not rear.

The Bride is ready to walk today
With flower girls ready to drop petals hooray.
Kaylee, Evie and Kaylann walk slowly down
The aisle and rose petals fall to the ground.

Cindy Dowell's harp playing warns all in view
That the Bride is about to make her debut.
The march begins and gasps are heard as they see
The Bride coming down the aisle so happy.

The vows are said as Bill Stone, expresses the vows.
They are repeated by the Bride and Groom, oh wow.
After a kiss and crying is finished done
Mr. and Mrs. Butler are presented as eternal one.

The ushers begin the process to leave
 With Mimi and other escorted out for all to see.
There were others who left as their turn came to be
And soon all had left, there were the Bride and Groom to see!

The four-wheeler was waiting for them – to get away!

James and Jennifer at their wedding blowing out the unity candle.

Their wedding napkins with their name and date!

This is the groom's cake. It is a tool box with tools around. All edible!

Jesus

There goes a man carrying a cross
Accused of what – I'm at a loss.
He healed the sick, the lame, the blind.
He loved those who had been treated unkind.

His words were kind and wise and true.
He fed five thousand with bread and fish of two.
He raised the dead and on water he walked;
Taught disciples and to crowds he talked.

He stumbles and staggers as he walks.
The cross is heavy, but he doesn't balk.
He is nailed to that cross as blood trickles down.
He even wears a painful thorny crown.

He cries before his last breath is through,
"Forgive them Father, they know not what they do."
It's over and done and then dark is the day
He's placed in a tomb expected to stay.

Three days pass, oh me, oh my!
Folks walk to the tomb and begin to cry,
"The stone is moved, and the body is gone!"
Somethings not right, something is wrong.

He appears to some here and there.
And for days He visits everywhere.
He is God's son and He bore our sin
To alter and change Satan's plan, my friend.

He suffered on that cross for you and me
All we need to do is have faith, you see.
Cause He forgives us of our sins, oh my!
So we can live with Him on high.

His love is abundant, of that I am sure.
He doesn't require perfection to endure.
He only asks for faith in all He's done
Because He is God's one and only son.

He walked this earth for thirty-three years.
He felt joy and pain with some tears.
He did not sin and was perfect each day,
So that He your price and mine could pay.

God's covenant with us is the key.
His son's blood covers us eternally.
How glorious in heaven life will be
With God in charge of all GLORY.

Jim & Kay

Each life is like a paper that's clean;
While each passer-by writes something unseen.
We know that we can certainly say;
That about the Robinsons, Jim and Kay.

During their stay at Horseshoe Drive,
The members and those quite new to arrive;
Had many fine things written each day,
By those special people, Jim and Kay.

Those things included such things as love,
Smiles, contentment and courage from above.
For those are the things that help others know,
Without much ado or even a show.

That God is in charge of everything,
And brings joy to those who regard Him as King.
Yes!!! The Robinsons known as Jim and Kay,
Have written good things during their Alexandria stay.

As we pass through this life time passes each day. We must remember that it takes time for God to grow His seeds within us. The pictures below took time, but God used the item to help each person involved to grow – according to his plans

Arbie Pugh Bowen was crowned Queen of the Nile. This dress was created & designed by Patricia Butler. We had 2 weeks to complete it so I enlisted the help of my friends. There are sequins all over the dress. The dress was put together by someone else after the sequins and beads were added.

Eddie Mc built this truck from parts gathered. He drove it to graduation practice and drove it after he joined the Navy.

Joyful Celebration

What a happy and joyful day is this date,
With family and friends here to celebrate.
The occasion is for a special someone
Named Dorothy Marie Vossel. What fun!

Her life has been filled with delight and despair,
As is with most folks who show that they care
About their loved ones and things they do.
Remember, all sunshine makes a desert, it's true.

Visions of a life filled ever with change
Come to mind as we ponder the amazing range
Of places lived from beginning to now
Of health issues fought and won, oh wow!

Born thirty October, Nanticoke, PA,
Into an economically depressed USA.
She married Fred Vossel, the love of her life,
Then became a delightful homemaker and wife.

They reared two boys named Rich and Fred.
She dared anyone to harm those she bred.
Joy comes to those who grow where planted,
And who accept life's offerings when slanted.

Dorothy accepted the changes life often threw,
But continually touched lives of those whom she new.
She supported her husband in every possible way;
While Fred's respect for her was the order of the day.

We thank her for touching each of our lives
And hope her life will continue to thrive.
With our hearts so filled we'd like to say,
"We hope this is a happy, happy, birthday!"

Dorothy Marie Vossel
Happy 85th Birthday!

Birthdate: October 30, 1926
85th Birthday Celebration: November 5, 2011
Community Banquet Room, American Bank and Trust
1450 Neal Street, Cookeville, TN 38501

Joy Giver

Debra Fox
(A Song Too!)

Leprosy, it was a dreaded disease,
In days of distant past.
And those who became infected.
Were soon despised outcasts.

I know that there are some people,
Who live in this world today,
Like lepers of past days,
Alone in outcasts ways.

Sinner, there is a fatal disease,
Caused by the deceiver of life.
His promises are without Jesus,
No love and eternal strife

My friend do you know my Jesus,
Or are you dying in sin?
For Jesus alone can save you.
And give you joy within.

Today there are many outcasts,
Without God's love that will last.
Who try to live in this world every day,
Without the Savior, "They say."

God hates the sin, loves the sinner,
He came to help us all see,
That He can heal the leper,
And He can save you and me.

Kaye Ryon

What a joy to know her these twenty-seven years.
Our friendship has grown through many joyful tears.
I first met her in our glorious choir room.
As she accompanied in preparation for us to sing soon.

She is a special lady in most every way.
A Christian with sensitivity always in play.
A wife, a mother, a sister, and a friend,
She touches lives from beginning to end.

Her gifts are numerous and talents too.
She has accompanied with the piano with many or few.
She has faithfully served whenever a need,
For orchestra, -ensembles, choir , and individuals, oh me!

Her profession was that of nursing, you know.
She has served her job well as her patients show,
And now she leaves to start a new life
In another place with family and less strife.

Her faith is strong wherever she goes.
Cause she isn't easily swayed as the wind blows.
Her responsibilities may change in every way,
But her life will be full as God directs each day.

Her faithfulness will be missed in Cookeville, that's true.
But her witness will live on to all those she knew.
Thank you God for allowing our life's paths to cross.
We know you have unbelievable plans for our special loss.

We wish you the best in every conceivable way.
Kaye Ryon, what else can we possibly say?
Except that we love you for your Christian way
Thank you! God bless you! Hip Hip Hooray!

> She played the piano for years, her husband and she decided it was time to retire and live with her children.

Lift Others Up

(A Song Too!)

Jesus never said you must be perfect.
Jesus only said believe in Me.
Folks may say you're wrong,
Judge you all along,
Tell you from your sins you can't be free.

But the Bible tells us all a different story
Like the woman at the well whose slate was clean.
And the Bible tells us all to love each other
Lift others up through their failures you have seen.

As we try to walk this daily pathway
As we try to do just what we should.
Satan comes to say, "Do it as I say"
You can't do what God wants anyway.

Do you feel down and really weary?
Do you feel that God just doesn't care?
Anguish in your heart.
Darkness won't depart.
You think sin has won the battle clear.

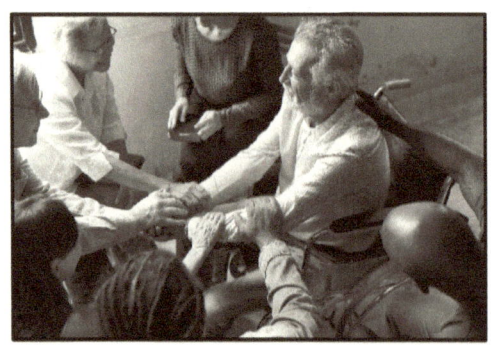

LISTENING

What do I do and what do I say?
There are so many things to address in a day.
We want to go here, we want to go there;
But what are we to do and we are to go where?

Are we to speak, to paint or even to sing?
Are we to play an instrument or build a giant of a thing?
Are we to listen to people with their life in a mess;
Or are we to wonder about philosophies that must be addressed?

Is it glamour and beauty and with all it entails?
Are we to pretend that all is correct, and no one fails?
Do we live without consequences in life each day,
And live with compromise every turn of the way?

Do we help in special ways--like others crossing the street?
Or do we visit a nursing home where new friends we meet?
Do we listen to students and children alike'
Who want someone to care and answer questions all night.

Do we sit by the bedside of those sick and dying each day?
Or do we listen to God as He tells us His way?
Only God can orchestrate our busy lives so fine,
To produce His will, His way, with His perfect time.

Love Letter To Our Parents

Our parents are people of whom we're quite proud;
However, we often don't say it out loud.
The tribute we give you on this special day;
To tell you just why we feel this way.
Words seem too simple for love such as yours;
However, we pray it will always endure.
You've raised us and listened to all of our noise.
You've spanked us and also bought us some toys.
You've watched us grow from wee to tall.
You've watched us learn things large and small.
You've endured our sorrow and suffered our pain.
You've watched us all of our animals tame.
You've traipsed us back and forth to school,
And taught us well the Golden Rule.
You've taught us that work was a joy not a pain,
And that life can be played as a wonderful game.
You've taught us to be fair in all that we do,
And to remember that God is always first too.
The list is so endless we really must say,
We are fortunate to have parents that are this way.
For life is an easier thing to live,
When we have parents such as you who give---
Those intangible qualities that make life worthwhile.
Now we hope to say in our own little style
That we love you dearly from the depth of our heart,
And from your teachings we will never depart.

William (Tom) Bowen
and Arbie Pugh Bowen

OBEDIENCE

WHAT HAS GOD CALLED <u>YOU</u> TO DO?
ARE YOU WEARY AND TIRED THRU AND THRU?
AS A CHRISTIAN, WHAT DOES HE WANT FROM YOU
TO QUIT OR KEEP ON GOING FOR WHAT IS TRUE?

DO YOU WONDER WHY OTHERS CAN'T SEE THE PLAN?
DO YOU WONDER WHY THEY CRITICIZE EVERY HAND?
IS IT A TEST TO SEE IF YOU'LL CONTINUE TO PROVE
THAT GOD WANTS OBEDIENCE NOT HUMANS TO APPROVE?

TELL OTHERS WHAT YOU PLAN TO DEFINITELY EXPLORE;
OR DREAMS THAT YOU SEE AT YOUR VERY CORE.
SOMETIMES YOU WONDER WHAT STEP TO TAKE,
SO YOU MOVE WITH FAITH AND HOPE YOU'RE NOT LATE.

OTHERS MAY CRITICIZE, COMPLAIN OR DISAGREE;
WHILE YOU ARE FOLLOWING GOD'S WILL OBEDIENTLY.
THINK ABOUT NOAH AND THE TAUNTS HE HEARD,
BUT HIS OBEDIENCE IS RECORDED IN GOD'S WORD.

THINK ABOUT RAHAB WHO HID GOD'S SPIES;
WHO WAS PROTECTED, AND HER FAMILY DID NOT DIE.
SHE IS ALSO RECORDED IN JESUS' LINEAGE, OH MY
OBEDIENCE IS DEFINITELY THE ANSWER FOR FAITH TO TRY.

WE MUST LISTEN TO HEAR FROM OUR LORD EACH DAY
AND FOLLOW HIS FOOTSTEPS AND ALWAYS OBEY.
IT MAY SEEM STRANGE OR EVEN OKAY
BUT WHATEVER IT IS WE MUST NOT DELAY.

HE MAY TELL YOU I'M COMING, BUT NOT TODAY;
OR HE MAY TELL YOU TO LISTEN AND SIMPLY OBEY
WHATEVER HE SAYS AND CONVEYS TO DO,
IS PERSONAL AND MEANT ONLY FOR <u>YOU</u>.

A cute replica of a mat to Patsey and Eddie in August 1975.
A Small Remembrance from Disney World.
Wish you could have been with us.
Love Mom and Dad

Our Oldest Son

Edward McNatt Butler II

The years had flown by rather quickly, you know
Married almost ten years with no children to show;
When the news soon arrived that an addition would be
Added to our family for all the world to see.

The long-awaited day arrived fi-nal-ly.
On 29 September 1976, a baby, oh me!
He was born to the Edward Butler family.
A boy with eyes of brown almost immediately.

The years have passed quickly as they do on this earth,
And 28 years have been used since his birth,
By God's grace and design from heaven above
He's grown in statue, knowledge, and love.

A father he's become with a daughter, Kaylynn.
With a wife to love and support him as a friend.
His business has become his strongest forte;
But sharing God's love has become his daily way.

From the day he arrived on this sinful earth
His parents have felt blessed by the gift of his birth.
Happy Birthday today and all of that stuff.
God's blessing on you in this life so tough.

Raejean, Teacher and Friend

Crying, growing, smiling, showing
New teeth, skinned knees knowing
That you are learning day by day
How to be an adult in future days!

School and graduation finally arrive.
Hopes and dreams are fully alive
With plans for college and God's design
To be a teacher of some kind.

By helping children to be all they can.
Teaching them of a Savior, a man,
Who loves all and has a purpose and plan.
For each individual born on this earth's land.

Not one graduation, but at least two
From a university called T. T. U.
Learning methods and neat ways to read
To help all ages or problems or needs.

Sharing with others what life provides
To make life better for those who reside
Within your path of friendship and love.
Directing your reasons to God above.

The years have sailed by quick as can be
From zero to the unbelievable forrrrrrr-ty!
What does the future hold in its hand?
Surprises, excitement with many a fan.

Cause in forty years you've a store
Of love for others and you're adored.
So continue to be a great teacher and friend.
And God will continue his love to send.

Raejean with her precious class being silly.

Seven Eleven Two Thousand Three
Kaylynn Danielle Butler

On seven eleven in the year two thousand and three
God introduced a precious child for all to see.
It was 12:38 or somewhere there about
When a baby girl was born, and all began to shout.

Her dad took her straight to the room where she lay,
For nurses to check her in every possible way.
Her mom soon entered exhausted but carrying a smile
Cause birthing her baby had taken a while.

The family that had waited was close to the door
And rushed to see her as their hearts did soar.
She had a head full of hair that was dark to the eye
And long fingers and nails that needed cutting, oh my!

Her parents proudly named her Kaylynn Danielle.
Now there are four generations living, that's swell
Her dad, his mom and her mom too;
Isn't that great and not always true.

Yet her mom and her mom's mom, and grandmother too
Were also all living at birth time wahoo.
Kaylynn was blessed to have so many
To love her at her very beginning.

Thank You
Johnathon Nelms

God sent a minister to our church in '93
To direct and teach music to the church's folks--like me.
It was clear that he came with the love of "I AM",
And believed that Jesus was the Sacrificial Lamb.

That first night I walked into choir and looked around,
And there he stood the newest man in our town.
He was tall and lean and a beard he did wear,
As he directed the choir that night with special care.

The days and months and years did go
With children's choirs, musicals, and Tebachiho.
Varied musical groups, dramas, and Christmas Programs anew
Filled the church with excitement and joy, it's true.

New educational degrees were earned in due time, hooray!
While the church continued to be blessed through God's vine each day.
Missions were always played with a very strong beat,
As Jonathan touched lives while sitting a Jesus' feet.

Seeking God's guidance, direction, and desires;
Whether leading instrumentalists, orchestra, or sanctuary choirs
Thank you Jonathan for your influence we can see;
And may God continue to bless your special ministry!

Fifteen years have passed since that very first night;
When the new man directed the choir with such delight
Isn't it a joy to know from the very start;
That if allowed God directs each part of our heart.

> He is such a wonderful individual and has helped me.

The Stranger

At Christmas time there was a man who looked so out of place,
As people rushed about him at a hurried sort of pace.
He stared at all the Christmas lights, the tinsel everywhere,
The shopping Santa Claus, with children gathered near.

The mall was packed with shoppers, who were going to and fro,
Some with smiles and some with frowns and some too tired to go.
They rested on the benches or they hurried on their way,
To fight the crowd for purchases to carry home that day.

The music from a stereo was playing loud and clear,
Of Santa Claus and snowmen, and funny-nosed reindeer.
He heard the people talk about the good times on the way,
Of parties, fun and food galore and gifts exchanged that day.

"I'd like to know what's going on," the man was heard to say
There seems to be some sort of celebration on the way.
And would you tell me who this is, all dressed in red and white?
And why are children asking him about a special night?"

The answer came in disbelief, "I can't believe my ear,
I can't believe that you don't know that Christmas time is here."
The time when Santa Claus comes around with gifts for girls and
boys, when they're asleep on Christmas Eve, he leaves them books
and toys.

The man you see in red and white is Santa Claus, so sly,
The children love his joyful laugh and twinkle in his eye.
His gift-packed sleigh is pulled along by very small reindeer,
As he flies quickly through the air, while darting there and here.

The children learn of Santa Claus while they are still quite
small, when Christmas comes he is the most important one of all!
The Stranger hung his head in shame, he closed a nail-pierced
hand, his body shook in disbelief, he did not understand.

A SHADOW CROSSED HIS STRICKEN FACE.
HIS VOICE WAS LOW BY CLEAR.
AFTER ALL THESE YEARS, THEY STILL DON'T KNOW....
AND JESUS SHED A TEAR.

"ONLY CHRIST LOVED US ENOUGH
TO DIE ON A CROSS FOR OUR SINS!!!"

Theme for Macau
Whatever

Whatever God wants we should be willing to do.
Habitually exhibiting the fruits of the spirit too.
Actually allowing God to work through us in all ways
Thanking and praising God for all things, every day.
Earthly natures should be put to death through prayer.
Voicing forgiveness for grievances of men everywhere.
Enjoying our circumstances whatever they be.
Remembering that gifts are to serve others we see.

This was taken at Sun Ya Sing Park. Sun Ya Sing was like the George Washington of China. He was a Christian! The two women are Nancy Caldwell and Patricia Butler.

Teaching in Macau.
Nancy Caldwell sitting down.
Ginger Massa standing.

Today

I passed a pitiful woman as I was walking down the street.
She wore tattered gloves and had a bag at her feet.
She didn't look as though she'd had a bath in several days,
And then I decided that I must be on my way.

I scurried down the street in a pace with normal beat,
And spoke to others as I passed or as we'd meet.
But I couldn't forget the woman that I'd earlier met,
And a picture appeared in my mind of fishing and a net.

A nudging in my heart encouraged me quite clear
That the woman with the bag was filled with pain and fear.
I felt my body turn and head from where I'd been,
Cause the woman with the bag was lost and filled with sin.

I hurried back to find her and saw multitudes of feet,
And then I saw a bag sitting by the curb on the street.
She was stooping to pick up food and eat it from the ground.
My heart was filled with tears when I heard those awful sounds

Of whips beating flesh and nails piercing hands,
And men casting lots for the clothes of a man.
Of a voice lifted toward heaven with words passionate and few
"Father forgive them for they know not what they do."

The unusual woman with the bag on the street
Needed love and help that I could surely meet.
Then the voice in my heart spoke these words to me,
"If you do it for the least of these you do it unto me.

I spoke to the woman who was standing on the street,
And learned she owned no possessions except the bag at her feet.
Then the voice in my heart said as plainly as could be
That you through His poverty might become rich indeed.

I asked the little woman to walk with me a spell.
I talked with her about the differences in heaven and hell.
She raised her eyebrow upward and with a toothless grin
She said my life is filled with nothing else but sin.

Do you really believe there is any hope for such as me?"
And I recalled Peter as he denied the Savior, not two times but three.
She looked me in the eye and with a sly little smirk.
Said I want to know this Savior whose love around me lurks.

My heart jumped flips as I heard a quiet voice within
Say, "Those cast the first stone, only those who are without sin."
I hugged the toothless woman and prayed to God above
To send this precious soul His unconditional love.

To heal her pain of loneliness and fill her physical needs.
His voice was very clear when I heard, "Who gives the sparrows feed?"
I heard the voice again as he said so quietly,
"Tell her of my mercy and my grace particularly."

God changed that precious soul right before my eyes.
As she picked up her bag and appeared extremely wise.
She opened her package and there in front of me
Was a Bible all tattered and frayed most pitifully.

What Is It About Christmas?

What is it about Christmas that makes us all so nuts?
Is it the gifts, the lights, the trees, or special cookie cuts?
What is it about Christmas that touches our hearts?
Is it the expressions on faces or music sung with parts.

What is it about Christmas that tugs at our soul
When children have no toys or soup in their bowl?
What is it about Christmas that causes tears on our face
When mangers and animals are seen in a place?

What is it about Christmas that unites folks each year
To create plays and dramas with music to hear?
What is it about Christmas that is your favorite part?
Is it the joy and feeling you feel in your heart?

What is it about Christmas that we really celebrate?
Is it the birth of Christ on this special date?
Or is it the love that Christ shared on this earth
That started that night of His special birth?

Whatever the reasons cause you to celebrate
Remember the purpose for this special date
Share Christ's love the entire year-round
As though He were there walking our ground.

Mother (Arbie Bowen). We celebrated Christmas at her house after my Grandfather died. She loved Christmas.

Who Is It?

He trudged down the road in a labored ole' way.
He was hoping that the war would end today.
He heard some shots that seemed far away,
And prayed for his buddies to be okay.

The cold in the air was much chill to bear,
And his gray tattered jacket had many a tear.
His boots had holes for the chill to creep in,
And he hadn't a blanket to help him, my friend.

He'd thought this war would be over and done.
Then in a few weeks life would be as it begun;
But, the war had hung on way too long.
Folks and land had been ravaged with many a wrong.

He had an old hat that still covered his head,
As though warmth could be there as he tread
Through the brambles, bushes, and wooded site
To find his buddies and help with the fight.

What was that sound he heard to the right?
Was it another soldier to join in the fight,
Or was it animals in the woods at daylight,
Or was it his hunger playing tricks of fright.

Then a burst of sound filled his being
A light from the right entered his seeing.
A pressure hit his body with a mighty force,
And he fell to the ground blood running its course.

He lay very still as he thought of his life.
His state, his farm, his children, his wife.
Would he see them again on this side of the river
Or would he die soon with a moan and quiver?

Later he heard someone approaching quietly,
For he heard a twig snap, leaves move and a bird flee.
It was a young boy carrying an old flint rifle
Dragging a body with tears—trying to stifle.

William Gibbs Butler

Excitement was growing on every hand.
A baby was to be born at Christmas time, oh man.
Ed's sisters were planning to celebrate in person to see.
The birth of this precious baby to be.

The family arrived at their usual time.
It was the 26th, and all seemed to be fine.
The next day was spent with everyone there.
Talking and enjoying the Christmas fare.

The next day started without much ado,
With Rhett and Adrienne getting anxious too.
Then suddenly a call came for all to hear.
The baby was making its way, it was clear.

Finally, the baby was born on December 28.
It was a boy with a nine-pound weight
He was also twenty-one inches long, they say
With blondish hair, what could go wrong?

That boy was named on that day
His name was William Gibbs Butler for all to say
And his parents were excited in every way
Cause God had visited them on that special day.

As all were seeing the baby so dear
Carly Beth was invited in to cheer.
She asked to hold her brother just born
Her dad said "Sit on my lap to hold the newborn."

She sang "Jesus Loves Me" to the new child
As those in the room cried through a big smile
The family that had once been three.
Was now a family with four for all to see.

Women of Wartimes

Even though meat was scarce to eat
Women had recipes for special treats;
Like mule tail soup with cotton berry pie;
Not necessarily great, but better than to die.

These elegant women showed endurance way beyond.
They endured cold, hunger, and dirt using their magic wand,
And faced the enemy with feminine appeal;
But became a wildcat with a moments deal.

Some homes were invaded for enemy heads,
Others invaded hospitals for the near dead.
Food was always a priority fare.
So kitchens were ravaged without a dare

Women and children were often thrown out of the house
To provide for themselves like a field mouse.
Regardless of their fate during the war,
They never gave up in the search for more.

Food, shelter, and medicine were in demand;
So women were used to helping on every hand;
Whether smuggling items in hair, hoop, wagon or shoe,
Women were cunning and served as spies too.

Yes, the men were warriors of the bravest sort,
They depended on home and land at every port.
Outnumbered and lacking medical relief,
They did better than Yanks in my belief.

Women of elegance and of tender grace,
Served life with a unique kind of lace;
Creativity, stamina, determination and love!
They fought their battle with guidance from above.

About The Author

Life is filled with roads that I have traveled but consider myself impaired or crippled by many factors. As a child I knew Jesus early and the human side of me spoke often. I thought that I knew what was best for me, but God had different roads for me to travel and different avenues for me to take.

It took several years to realize that God knew so much more than I did and that the human side of me knew nothing. Let me begin with teaching. It is and was my passion, But I did not know it for a while. As an example, I was President of the Future Teachers Club in my High School and I didn't realize I was going to be a teacher.

I had a Bachelor's Degree from Southwestern at Memphis, now called, Rhodes, and a Masters' Degree from Memphis State University. I taught music for eight years while living in Memphis. It was a great experience, and I traveled many avenues during that time.

I met my husband during that adventure. After a few years John Deere hired him and we moved to Malden, Missouri for training time and then to Alexandria, Louisiana, for seventeen years. During that time, I taught Kindergarten, taught music at a private school, taught class piano, taught private piano, taught handicapped children, was teacher of the year for my district and had three boys. WOW!!!

God had plans for me I hadn't even thought about. He taught me many things during that time, and I traveled many, and I mean many roads, I had not intended to travel.

I have traveled for the school boards where I have been and gained many thoughts, I would not have experienced, but I knew that the one in charge of the universes was always there.

Then, my husband decided to quit John Deere. So, we were located in Cookeville, Tennessee. What did God have in store for me now? Once again, He provided. I taught at the Alternative School. Mr. Marcus Durley was the Principal, and he ran the school by his rules. He was wise beyond his years and taught me many things about discipline.

The school was high school students who needed someone to care or they were lazy, or they did not care. Although it was a great learning adventure, I felt that I was a value to the students. Then I realized that I needed to be there for my family in other ways, so I took a school teaching position to help that situation.

I taught Resource students. As it turned out, I handled many behavior problems that made a difference in those students. The students themselves were my advocates and helped me many times to touch the lives of those rebelling.

I did not plan to travel the Special Education route, but I did. God often uses coincidences to create a plan. He did that for me. If He will do that for me, He will do that for anyone because I was a crippled person, who had a plan for my life. That is too funny when I think about it NOW!!!

God has always lifted me up beyond my ability and touched others through my work. I pray that the poems touch your heart in such a way that God is glorified and that you know Him as your personal Savior. Only He can make your life more.

Edward & Patricia Butler.
We were married for ten years and then had three sons.

Message From The Publisher

What you have in your hands is not by coincidence, nor was it put together for any other purpose than to encourage and share through words; that not only is God real, but He wants to be active in our lives. It is amazing how He can take someone's life like Patricia Butler's and mine use it to influence so many people.

Every one of these poems is connected to at least 1 other person, and a majority includes up to 4 people at a time. I learned that God would use whatever He deems necessary to fulfill His plan. In the end, every decision He (God) makes is for our own good because God loves us.

As we sat down to discuss how we were going to put these poems together into one Book, it first appeared to be a large task. As it turned out, it was one of the easiest books we have published to date. Not because of its size (less than 75 pages) but as we were laying the book out, I discovered that through these poems I found myself reflecting on my life. Seeing just how much in common we all have through God's eyes. These poems in which the Author, Patricia Butler wrote, will tell you that it was God who wrote them Through Her.

Prior to writing this page, we (my wife and I) prayed that whoever God saw fit to hold this beautiful book (YOU), that God would bless YOU with a super abundance of Joy, and out of a grateful heart and with thanksgiving to Him (God) who, providing with such a blessing, that you will order as many copies as the Lord leads you, and cheerfully you will share it with those you love.

Poem Index
(Alphabetically)

After Thoughts Related to Macau 6
An Apprentice 7
Angels 8
Baby Dyer 9
Calamity 10-11
Carly Beth Butler 12
Christian Fruits 13
Dominica 14-15
Do We Look For Another 16
Do You Know My Savior 18-19
Evelyn Mae Butler's Birth 20
Faith 21
Fifty Years 22-23
From The Heart 24
Gifts 25
Gordon Who? 26
Grains of Sand 28-29
Happy Birthday Adrienne Smith Butler 30-31
Happy Birthday Rhett Butler 32
Heaven's Gift of Love 33
I'm Just A Sinner Saved By Grace 34-35
James Lee Butler & Jennifer Foust's Wedding 36-37
Jesus 38-39
Jim and Kay 40
Joyful Celebration 42-43
Joy Giver 44
Kaye Ryon 45

Lift Others Up	46
Listening	47
Love Letter To Our Parents	48
Obedience	49
Our Oldest Son	51
Raejean, Teacher and Friend	52-53
Seven Eleven Two Thousand Three	54
Thank You	55
The Stranger	56-57
Theme For Macau Whatever	58
Today	60-61
What Is It About Christmas	62
Who Is It?	64-65
William Gibbs Butler	66
Woman of Wartimes	67
About The Author	68-70
Message From The Publisher	71

For God So Loved The World,
That He Gave His Only Begotten Son.
WHOSOEVER believes in Him
Shall Not Perish
But Have Eternal Life.

John 3:16

www.ingramcontent.com/pod-product-compliance
Lightning Source LLC
Chambersburg PA
CBHW030916080526
44589CB00010B/324